THE BREAKFAST MACHINE

Helen Ivory was born in Luton in 1969, and lives in Norwich. She has worked in shops, behind bars, on building sites and with several thousand free-range hens. She has studied painting and photography and has a Degree from Norwich School of Art.

In 1999 she won a major Eric Gregory Award from the Society of Authors; in 2005 she was given an Art's Council Writer's Award, and in 2008 an Author's Foundation Grant. She has published three collections with Bloodaxe Books: *The Double Life of Clocks* (2002), *The Dog in the Sky* (2006) and *The Breakfast Machine* (2010).

She has taught creative writing for Continuing Education at the University of East Anglia for nine years and has been Academic Director there for five. She is an editor for the Poetry Archive, a tutor for the Arvon Foundation and is currently studying for a PhD in Creative and Critical Writing at UEA.

HELEN IVORY

THE BREAKFAST MACHINE

BLOODAXE BOOKS

ISBN: 978 1 85224 873 4

First published 2010 by
Bloodaxe Books Ltd,
Highgreen,
Tarset,
Northumberland NE48 1RP.

www.bloodaxebooks.com
For further information about Bloodaxe titles
please visit our website or write to
the above address for a catalogue.

Supported by
**ARTS COUNCIL
ENGLAND**

Cover design: Neil Astley & Pamela Robertson-Pearce.

Printed in Great Britain by
Bell & Bain Limited, Glasgow, Scotland.

To the chickens, and to Martin, always

ACKNOWLEDGEMENTS

Acknowledgements are due to the editors of the following publications in which some of these poems first appeared: *A Clock-Storm Is Coming* (Cinnamon Press, 2006), *Ambit*, *Arty 23*, *Horizon Review*, *Magma*, *Multilingual Matters*, *nth Position*, *Poetry Salzburg Review*, *Seam* and *Stride online*. 'The Story of Light' was written for the Voicing Visions Exhibition (a collaboration with the Norwich 20 Group.)

I would also like to thank Neil Astley, Martin Figura, Jo Guthrie, Andrea Holland, Matthew Howard, Andrew McDonnell, Esther Morgan, Andrea Porter, Penelope Shuttle, George Szirtes and Padrika Tarrant.

CONTENTS

Hold on to the wind with your teeth.

SERBIAN PROVERB

The End of the Pier Show

With a magician's wrist,
she summoned flowers
from inside her coat,
silk scarves and rabbits,
so many rabbits.

A snap of her fingers
and a flame rose
from the palm of her hand,
she clapped and the shape of a cat
curled in her arms,

became tiger, circled her legs,
became fire and tiger,
paced around her,
became ten feet tall,
threw shadows to the front of the stage.

Music ripped from the throats
of a million songbirds
bled into the fusty air of the theatre
where three rows from the back
a little girl stood up, put down her doll.

The Dolls House

The trees that grow
from the nursery walls
do not rustle in the breeze
of an open window.

The jaws of the wardrobe
do not snap shut
when a crane-fly bumbles
into their waiting smile.

But there is a shifting of furniture
in the dolls house tonight,
a slow dragging of objects
across candle-lit rooms.

The kitchen windows steam up
and the unmistakable smell
of melting plastic
drifts from the chimney.

You will notice tomorrow
your new doll is gone.
You will find her blonde hair
lines a mouse nest in spring.

The Tooth Mouse

All of the teeth
bought by the Tooth Mouse
are piled up in an out-of-town
warehouse

They are gnashing
and grinding
and want to return
to the mouths of sleeping children.

It is said that they are whiter
than bone, cleaner
than melt-water, more innocent
than the children themselves.

But look at them here
all broken and angry,
chewing at the cold
metal door to get out.

Sleep

In this house, everything sleeps.
Even the walls have relaxed
and the roof is too tired
to hold up the weight of the sky.

It is so long since the front door
has opened, the skin has grown over.
The postman has given up
looking for the letter-box.

The girl in the room upstairs
is a woman now. In waking moments,
she sleepwalks to the mirror,
takes a brush to the long silk of her hair.

Before she lies down again, she'll notice
the bird skulls on the window-sill,
how cobwebs have laced them together,
how her face has grown sharp as a knife.

Marks

She paints bone black on her arms
where he held her,
on the ridge of her pelvis,
cinnabar on her breasts, thighs
and on her lips like a balm.

She throws herself on a white linen sheet,
lets it absorb her pigments.
Her lips trace a pattern of wordless shapes,
like the dust left by a moth
in the palm of a hand.

How to make a pot of tea

Take a bowl of weed from the sea,
plunge in your hands, wrists,
then up to the elbows.

Soon you are wading, you are waist-deep
and before you know it
you are living underwater.

Time passes. You have a new job,
have taken up different hobbies,
have learned to burn sea-coal to warm yourself.

More time passes, and your life has become
a series of complicated pretends, and you imagine
you were born here; were brought up in a family of part-fish.

Then you find the syringe
in the pocket of your old coat. It's filled with air
that wants to bubble into your veins.

When you climb from the bowl
you leave a puddle of water on the kitchen floor.
You fill up the kettle and forget to turn off the tap.

Unbidden

Somehow the stork,
has left a tiny bloody
hairless form beside
the vegetable patch.

This creature belongs
inside. It would be happy
with the kittens
in their basket.

The sun-baked earth
begins to tear
with a cry so deafening,
all the windows shake.

She hides inside
the linen cupboard
among the deep wash
of bleach, the crisp of starch.

The mother cat licks
her babies clean as bone.
Dark red smearing
the corners of her mouth.

Creation

On the third day, she draws the sun
into her mouth and swallows it whole.
It glows in her throat, sinks down
to her stomach, bubbles through
her insides, like molten gold.

On the fourth day, she lets the moon
enter her, plant its seed in her womb,
grows its silver children, till strong enough
to swim into the nightlong sky,
and take their place among the heavens.

On the fifth day she takes the sea into her hands,
runs it through her fingers like silk.
She puts fishes into coral baskets for her children;
waits from them to haul them up
to fill their greedy mouths.

On the sixth day, she cuts her skin
with her own sharpened nails, drips blood
into deep black earth, falls to her knees.
She watches trees and animals grow up
from the ground as she becomes weaker.

On the seventh day, she is barely breathing.
She hears the postman and the phone
that keeps ringing. She is aware of a light,
which she thinks is the sun, burning her eyes.
For two days, for two days, she rests.

Luck

Your black cat has been gone for days.
He returns to you now
with sooty paws,
smirches your fresh swept floor.

You are making risotto with mushrooms
collected from the park, you are
de-inking calamari with a dexterous knife,
you are grinding spices.

But when you run the bath,
outside disappears.
When you run the bath,
it's like a well, filling up, filling up.

Right at the bottom you see
your face swimming in red clouds.
Gentle at first, beautiful.
And then you climb in.

When you climb in
the colour rises like a fever
and your pale skin is flushed
with the heat of your own blood.

The bathroom door unpaints itself,
floorboards tick like a clock,
dark blooms creep up the walls,
the water begins to cool.

Cypher

Her weight suspended in air
casts no shadow on the wooden floor.
Light spills from the open window,
spells out the shape of her face,
the line of her arms, belly,
the ridge of a scar, her hands.

This is pure language,
played from frame to frame
until a complete sentence is constructed,
making sense of all this unused space.
Still this chill passes over her,
presses its fingers to her neck, counts her pulse.

Migration

The sky's starlings
are outside her window,
bustling the branches of a tree.

She didn't ask for them,
doesn't know their names;
still they are calling hers.

ou asked what I was afraid of

I am caught in a storm
with the whole ocean of sky above me
being whisked into a giant meringue.

There is a card game, just off set
and the seven and three of hearts
are whipped into the mixing.

They bleed and leave a clot
like a fertilised egg in the clouds and I am watching
this spectacle from the side of a road.

From the far hills, an ant writ large
brings its silhouette closer
to reveal you as an unsaddled rider on its back.

The sound of you reciting the first twenty elements
of the periodic table over and over
in the voice of a bull

would be the last thing I hear
as a card flips over,
revealing itself to be Alexander the Great, no less.

Notes from the Garden

Most days he is rootless and troubled
and feels his heart in his chest
like a boot-full of chickens
on their way to the market.

She has learnt to keep out of the way;
to eat oranges as tidily as she can;
releasing their sweetness
standing over the sink.

Nights he is upright as a knife
moon or no moon,
watching fireflies dance above
whatever bonfire he has made.

The clock is two moons

on a badly inked sky
and time drips down the wrists
of the clock-maker.
For the want of a seven
he's turned a two upside down.

As he wanders away
he is whistling a song
that belonged to his father.
And the clock clicks its tongue
the way only clocks can.

Record

A man enters a house
on a reel of foxed film
to the sound
of a cine-projector.

He shaves into a broken mirror
as a clockwork hen's
mechanism unwinds
till she ceases to eat.

And in the next room
an endless sharpening of pencils,
as the film catches fire
on its way through the gate.

Birdcage

Do you not hear the music
from the birdcage of feathers
strung high up in that tree?

Every now and then a squirrel
uses clever fingers to rewind, press play,
so we can believe in birdsong.

Even the squirrel, though,
is losing faith in this charade.
His eyes no longer sparkle.

His coat weighs heavy on his back,
and if some quick knife
could free him from it, he'd be grateful.

Horsemen

In this, the dawn of the apocalypse
the cowboys have itchy fingers
as they ride into the centre of town.

Not a squeak can be heard
from the people that live here,
though a dog howls, chained up in a yard.

A game of cards sits unplayed
on a kitchen table. The winner
hides under a bed, unsure of his hand.

Jumble Sale

Toys are lost from their boxes
and upside down,
jigsaw puzzles
will not make sense
and none of the shoes
have laces.

On a table in the middle
two figures wrestle,
all arms and legs.
Over in bric-à-brac,
a doll with no eyes watches
from behind kitchen scales.

Making Rain

It's always summertime in the cellar
and the chickens are chattering softly
to each other about the impossibility
of this, and other things.

When the light-bulb blows
and no one comes to replace it
they'll look like they've been plucked alive
if anyone could see them.

So when the villagers shoot at clouds
and the unstoppable rain comes
they will be already suitably goose-fleshed
and chilled through to their hearts.

Safe-house

Residents are ghosts;
sheet-covered
in every room.

Figures in armchairs
television news blazing,
sheets barely moving as they breathe.

In the kitchen,
a woman's drape
marries her to the oven.

Upstairs, the sleeping forms
of children bedded down
for a long night.

Dust and ash fall inexplicably
not touching a soul.

In That House

Every floorboard is a tip-off,
every door a squealer,
the telephone has your number.

The people that live there
have sewn buttons to their lips
but to still a heart-beat is harder.

Only the cellar
holds silence like an egg
in a tank of dark water.

After Hours

At night the mannequins
come alive in the basement

and the ones in the window
unhitch all their clothes.

In their new state
they are unshod and sexless

and when the conductor
(a demiurge in spangled jacket)

taps his baton
they all sing with one voice.

Slot Machine

People are pebbles
and windows are mirrors.

When the moon is pushed
down the chimney's throat,
the music begins.

So the pebbles dance
a formal little dance,
learned through generations.

Looking out the window
they see their reflection.

They think the whole world
is dancing.

Stones

The cluster of stones
round the door

had journeyed all night
just to tell us their story.

But daylight had sutured
their mouths

and their hearts were buried
in their grey insides.

We tried to feed them milk
from a silver bowl.

At dusk, they just picked up their shadows
and dragged them away.

The Orange Seller

A woman on the bus
is selling oranges;
mouldy little oranges
with no juice inside.

Yet people are buying them
and peeling them
with a grim-faced
determination.

She is shoeless,
and chirrups
like a ragged little bird.
And still we buy her oranges.

Her hands are outstretched,
as if expecting rain.

Magicians

They think the world
is found in their pocket
if they just pull out
enough scarves.

They think doves
are for their sole amusement,
that rabbits are content
to live under their hat.

They keep the halved bodies
of all their mistakes
in cellars, with the bloodied
sequins and boas of their trade.

They think they know
what you're thinking;
the card you hold
close to your chest.

Mouse Trap

This house is only part constructed;
the absence of roof, walls even,
the lack of privacy in the red plastic bath,
is what we have grown to expect.

We are mice here, scuttling through
dark corridors in each other's heads.
We are trappers, too; dragging in
paraphernalia from the outside world

to build the perfect trap. A shoe, a bucket,
a diving-board and a man poised to dive;
the clattering sound of a metal ball
rolling down rickety stairs.

When the mouse is caged at the end of the game,
the other mice, who are trappers squeak
with a glee so loud it could waken the dead;
thanking all their lucky stars. And so it goes.

Office Block

The palace of windows is burning tonight
and the city is the colour of amber.

Firemen scale the impossible walls
to rescue rats and spiders.

The staircase that curls like a shell
makes a fine spectacle

as if this were the flaming stairway
to all hell itself.

To the very hell that turns glass
into piles of sand that must be swept

and swept again, and still again
forever through windy corridors.

Bedtime Story

The man trapped inside his body
hears his heart pound
like a hot little mouse on a wheel.

Too many snakes squirm
in the dark well of his belly.
He feels his liver grow cell by cell.

So he begins to live inside his head
in the clean-cut world of numbers
as drawn by a digital clock.

At night he sings facts to himself like lullabies
and pushes the heavy boat of his body
into the empty and chemical dark.

Moon

The spine of this tower block
is breaking.
My heart too, is suddenly lame
as it shuffles around
the walls of my chest
like a grey dog
unable to settle.

I am calling across hills
and meadows
of broken-down cars.
I am shouting, and my mouth
is as wide as a river,
and my voice is as loud
as a hatful of headaches.

The sky is a sheet
of black paper,
and the moon is painted
with the brush of a child.
With the same brush
he takes, and he loads,
and then skilfully paints out the stars.

Night-time at the Office

The solitary light
at the top of the office block
way after midnight
where a hand in the darkness
stamps yesterday's date
on letters that will never be sent.

There is nothing here
but the buzz of the light
and the soft fluttering of moth.
A pile of letters teeters
on the edge of the desk,
their recipients, sound in their beds.

The Reckless Sleeper

All night he has been inventing a vocabulary –
a mythology of cities built like a circuit board;
a skeletal picture of where he'd like to belong.

He is wrapped in a blanket of grey paint,
and sometimes an apple will roll to the surface,
sometimes a mirror, or an apple in the mirror.

Sometimes a lion will lift a lazy paw
and pull the blanket from the other side of the bed;
leaving him exposed to the dark of the room.

He walks on the surface of heaven,
he holds his own heart in the palm of his hand,
his eye is a metronome; candle, bird, candle, bird.

Staircase Game

At the bottom, a man plays dice
with the knuckle bones of sheep.

Soon, he will eat his shoelaces;
twirl them round his fork like spaghetti.

At the top, after a long night of waiting,
the birth of winged horses

to the sound of trumpets
and the shifting of a hundred wings.

A glass of honey sits untouched
on the middle step.

Its sweetness is all
you'll be asked to remember.

Fish Allegory

Sun in the desert sky
like a half-sucked sweet

and fish swims circles
round the suitcase in his bowl.

Fish thinks of four numbers.
By and by, the suitcase opens;

reveals a kinder sky,
the silver thread of river.

The suitcase closes
with fish inside.

Now the bowl boils like a kettle,
but the whistle is fish's own.

The Story of Light

(after Louise Richardson)

Let me tell you the story of light
and all it can show you;
how it keeps night away
with a long forked stick.

Let me tell you of candles,
of firelight, of angels
and their flight through darkness;
their messages of light.

What happens next is your choice
though the moon that I've painted
has calm seas,
warm enough to dive into.

My love, I have walked this path
so very long that the soles of my feet
mirror the sky, and I have almost forgotten
what I used to be called.

If you come with me,
I will show you the earth wound up
in a neat little ball.
I will tell you my name.

Eclipse

A man holds a white flag to the sky
and the moon catches fire
in earth's shadow.

    *

Here the rain has been falling
for a thousand years without pause
or even a flicker of doubt.

    *

A town at night on a hill,
a television after closedown,
its high-pitched wail, its splashy glitter.

    *

A man stands next to a sun-warm rock,
he dreams of water, sees water spring
from the rock, cups his hands.

Cutting Grass

A question is asked
deep in the earth,
out of earshot
of anything animal.

After an epoch of rain,
there's an answer
ready, on the tips
of the tongues of grass.

Handstand

After the deafening mad rush of blood,
after the glittered shapes
have cleared from your eyes,
you settle into the pose of a tree
roots exposed to the sunlight.

Your spine is already too tightly packed,
the weight of yourself
crushes you to the ground.
Pretty soon, your skeleton will calcify,
and your useless roots will dry out.

Then, rich music will sing from the earth
until your whole body resonates
with amber tones. Your leaves will die
without light, and earthworms
will embroider you into the soil.

Undeliverable

Most likely there is a network problem that prevented delivery,
but it is also possible that the computer is turned off.

I have seen the mailbox in the Florida heat,
the grass around it charred beyond redemption.
I have heard the words of God,
spat out in tongues of fire.
I understand if you choose not to believe me.

I understand in this day and age, that light
is the neon glow spilling out into the skies
above cities and towns.
It is the radiance of a small screen
bleeding into the dark of your room.

But what if the words you send flailing into space
do not ricochet from lonely satellites
back into your lap, like unwanted stars?
What if they are held by the gravity of another world;
become burning towers, firebirds even?

Prague, the Kafka Café

Let me first describe the room –
walls made of smoke,
ceiling not there,
save the weight of the floor above.

The waitress at the bar,
has no eyes for customers.
She brings her boyfriend coffee
with three sugar cubes.

A spiral staircase winds down
like a snake, leads you
to the heart of the city, where rats
collect treasures in their nests.

Lunch is cold potato soup
and the taste of burnt fat
will sit in your stomach all day,
like a bowl of sump oil, threatening to tip over.

Tea Party

It was a tea-party like any other tea-party,
the tide was way out, and the table
up to its knees in black glacial sand.

Alice and the White Rabbit shakily balanced
on beach-balls, inched closer to the empty chairs
that sat either side of me and the sleepy mouse.

White noise from an invisible waterfall
seemed to hide inside china cups
like sea in a shell if I put my ear to them.

You were nowhere to be seen, but your voice
bumped round the walls of my skull,
left soggy cake crumbs in the dregs of my tea.

Confectionery

A man lies in the dark
and the clock hands out time;
a child apportioning sweets.

In the man's pile, candy
sticky and medicinal,
hard enough to break your jaw.

In the child's pile
gobstopping eyeballs
stare out into sugar-paper black.

World

A single blond kitten
bundled into a sack
weighted with stones
and thrown into the lake.

So winter begins
and the moon floats
to the surface
of the part-frozen water.

And nothing but
the trigonometry of stars
keeps things together,
keeps them apart.

Puppet

Look at you, darling puppet
all snug in your box –
it's high time you kicked up your heels,
now the nights are drawn in.

I'll send you out like a bad mother,
with the path impossibly narrow
and the trees bound to snag your strings –
best to ignore those anonymous howls.

Fear not child, your heart is made of wood
after all; you are a meal for no beast.
And the strings, if you look, are gone
the light from my window grown weak.

Listen

There really is nothing
in the corridor of teeth
but a slash of light.

And though
from the kitchen
a clattering of pans

and the nervous cackle
of a single hen
winds its way to your ears,

be hushed, my love, be calm
or some piebald bird
will pluck out your tongue.

Chamber

Once in the whole history of darkness,
a whirring contraption of metal and plastic
took on the shape of a bird.

When it found it could fly
when it found it had no heart-beat
it lifted itself into the night like a howl.

Later, it swooped down to land,
fed on the souls escaping,
and souls too snared to move an inch.

Light came in sheet flashes,
insisted pictures through the eye of the bird,
drove deep into what passed for its heart.

The Breakfast Machine

Behind a wood sliding door
the whistling and grinding
of a great machine
brings us slowly, inexorably
towards breakfast.

Even the keenest eyes
of the imagination,
will not inform you
what kind of alchemy
is at work there.

The chicken is the thing
that troubles me most,
as she crosses the kitchen
on squeaky tin legs
emerges at the serving hatch

cocks her head to one side,
takes in the room
with the bead of an eye
shrieks out with a voice
like grating glass:

Scrambled, poached, boiled,
scrambled, poached, boiled.

The Beginning

When they nailed the cabinet shut,
the rabbit knew it was quite dead
Innards and eyes were replaced
by straw and glass,
its heartbeat had become a rustling.

When it tried to drag itself
from the mounting,
its hide shredded like paper,
but still it climbed up on two legs,
kicked open the door with new cloven hooves.

The crepuscular light of the workshop
hinted at other creatures
trapped in glass boxes.
In each one, a shifting
of fur or scales, the glint of a claw.

The key to the door was easy to find,
so the rabbit unlocked it.
Slipping a dark cloak
around his shoulders,
he trotted into the high street.

Across the road, a fish with wings
played the accordion
in the shelter of a shop door
and a cat with the face of a bird
was scanning a newspaper.

The streets were filled with people
on their way home from work,
too busy to notice the newborn dead in their midst,
following the rabbit in slow procession
towards the freshly built structure of ribs and human hair.

Dolls

This one's child has emptied her tears
into its heart and turned it to salt.
Poor salt doll,
there's no end to her sorrows.

*

There's always someone to do your dirty work,
always someone
with plucked-out eye,
with snapped-off hands.

*

A froufrou legion
with wide-awake eyes
in the junkshop window,
they have all lost their names.

*

Made of wax
they will inherit the earth
if that's what you want –
there's all manner of spells.

A Little Spell in Six Lessons

(after Ana Maria Pacheco)

You must first mask
your human self,
then forget your tongue.
Learn to talk as birds
or cloven hoofed things.

*

To lose yourself
is a very particular art.
If you want ever to be found
scatter breadcrumbs,
pray the birds are not hungry.

*

I will tell you a story
of the dark corners
that hold us in place,
of the chandelier of bones,
the wind whistling through teeth.

*

Your body is a sheet
of blank paper
and the birds have eaten
their fill of your path.
They have pecked out your eyes.

*

Now see afresh,
see what you've become!
Your words are butterflies
pinned to your tongue –
release them.

*

And what you hold
is perhaps what you wished for
as you sang as a child
in your feathered chair
when the world was asleep.

Wish

Talk soft to me,
talk gently as the night
shuffles its papers
in high offices and hilltops.

Talk low like cattle,
breathe hay-scented words
and I will show you the book
kept inside my coat,

already learnt by heart
by the nightjars that churr
to each other before daylight
setting the darkness home.